I0464367

Bryan Healey

START-UP STRUGGLES

Copyright © 2014 by Bryan Healey
ISBN 978-1500927004
www.healeyengineering.com

All rights reserved.

No part of this book may be used or reproduced in
any manner whatsoever without written
permission, except in the case of brief quotation
embodies in critical articles and reviews.

For information:
Bryan Healey at bryan@bryanhealey.com

Printed in the USA

"I think that's the single best piece of advice: constantly think about how you could be doing things better and questioning yourself."

Elon Musk
CEO, Tesla and SpaceX

INTRODUCTION

The start-up is a magical thing...

With the great successes of the last few decades, from Steve Jobs to Bill Gates to Elon Musk, it is too easy to focus on the potential financial benefits of the start-up exercise, but the magic is so much more than just money and fame.

It's about doing something uniquely you!

The computer revolution has created an amazing and unparalleled level of opportunity for those with an entrepreneurial spirit, those who dare to dream. The barrier to entry has been greatly reduced, and it keeps dropping everyday. If you have the idea, the passion, and the risk tolerance, there is almost no idea out there that you aren't able to pursue.

But there is always some struggle...

In all my years of working for, and occasionally starting (some successfully, some unsuccessfully), a number of start-ups in and around the Boston area, I have experienced a number of persistent issues that seem to pervade the entire start-up world. I've heard these same struggles from so many others from so many industries and places and times. And so, I will talk a bit about these struggles, and offer what I've learned in dealing with each. I can only hope I am able to help you avoid a little pain as you work in the most invigorating, exciting, adventurous, and unique experience in modern civilization!

Let's build something together...

QUICK TIPS

1. Always challenge your assumptions
2. Don't be afraid to change
3. Listen to your team
4. Trust your gut, but support with data

THE IDEA

It's common for those with technical or managerial skills to say they have interest in entrepreneurship. The perceived benefits of controlling your very own company are vast and ingrained: freedom from the corporate doldrums, a flexible schedule, a rounded and directed life, a cause for the caring heart, and the possibility of vast riches. These benefits have generated interest that has gained even greater traction and fervor in recent years as many post-bubble internet ventures have begun seeing colossal and very public successes (and the great multitude of failures have gone tragically unreported). With amazing consistently, nearly every time one of these companies goes public or is acquired, bathing the founding team and investors in great wealth, I hear people repeat: "I could have done that!" It is the recitation of the greatest fallacy, as old as the world itself, that the best idea is what wins.

It isn't...

...okay, fine, *sometimes* it is...

But it's still very rarely the idea that breeds the victory. Rather, it is all in the execution, the ability to adapt to external pressures with quickness and grace, and a resilient and unstoppable management team that creates the eventual victory. That original idea is merely the launching point in which those with like-minded vision and passion come together for a common cause. It is not at all unusual for that team to pivot, to change directions at a later point, redirecting their joined efforts towards a completely unrelated (or loosely related) objective, and pursue that new idea with equal vigor. You need to be ready to change and evolve! If you are depending on a single brilliant idea to reach success, then you are not making yourself available to opportunity.

Now, I'll exercise some caution and say that, like all things in the start-up world, nothing is an absolute. There is something to be said for the careful application of steadfast determination, for unwavering focus in the face of adversity, and for a strategic vision that ignores the environmental noises of the market. Many great companies and product lines have been birthed out of the roiling cauldron of uncertainty; imagine a world in which Apple succumbed to loud claims of the impossible in digital rights management and never went into the music business. There are times when a founder must decide to stay the course, to keep the team focused on a path of uncertainty, and to try to realize a larger vision. But it is an important (and, unfortunately, a largely intangible) attribute of the successful entrepreneur to be able to recognize the difference between the truly impossible and the merely very difficult.

The best method I have found for keeping track of your vision, and for uncovering any need to pivot, is to listen. The best entrepreneurs surround themselves with an army of official and unofficial mentors and advisors; they talk about their vision and their company with openness and honesty, harboring a genuine desire for criticism. They don't want yes-men, they want coaches and belligerents; they want to be challenged, to be forced to defend their vision and to find any weaknesses not yet considered. And they talk regularly with their team and their investors and their customers, they keep tabs on progress and setbacks, and they entertain all recommendations with an open mind.

Keep a notebook with you at all times, and take tireless notes (always keep track of the date). Be aware of what the market is doing. Know your competition thoroughly, know your industry well, and know your customer as if they represented your very health and vitality. Subject your products and services to rigorous testing and analytical coverage, and get any needed changes in front of real users as quickly as possible. Have an easy and intuitive way to receive user feedback (a bottom or side button for feedback is a common solution). Always be seeking more information, more analysis, more criticism; it takes a sound and brutal beating before you can get back up and win the fight.

And always remember: The original idea is not your greatest asset. Your mind, your network, and your team are your greatest assets. Use them.

QUICK TIPS

1. Look for another founding member
2. Lean hard on advisors and mentors
3. Be cautious with equity
4. Move fast but smart

TECHNICAL CO-FOUNDER

There is probably no time more critical, stressful, and dangerous than when a non-technical founder is looking to hire the first engineer. Expanding a team has an elegant simplicity to it, assuming you use established tactics for identifying compatible new hires. But it's rarely easy to get that first engineer in the door unless you already own a deep and broad professional network. When you're alone in a room with a white board, it can be easy and exciting to engineer a product, to layout the basic workflow, to imagine your customers at play. But when it is time to put that idea to code, you'll need to dip into your pockets (or equity) and seek out an adventurous engineer to be the technical co-founder.

So, what do you look for?

The same general rules of any hiring process still apply, but there are some additional attributes that are important to find in a technical co-founder. First and foremost, you will need to think of this first hire as the last addition to the founding group rather than the first addition to the team; a technical co-founder is still a co-founder, and must exhibit the same entrepreneurial spirit as everyone else. In the early days, this person will shoulder a tremendous amount of work for shockingly little pay (or equity-only), and should represent the future of technical leadership as the company (hopefully) grows. It can be tempting to assign work to a contract engineer, and under special circumstances that could be appropriate, but I highly recommend trying to find someone with passion and buy-in, who will struggle alongside you when times get lean and frustrating.

You will also want someone with a bit of full-stack knowledge (whatever stack that may be). A product is built in code, of course, and that needs to be where this person makes their living. But you are not likely to have any operations, quality assurance, database, or design staff for quite some time, and you want someone who can develop all the initial architecture with at least passable competence to minimize total cost. This person will not be merely a member of the development squad, they are not a code monkey; they will represent all the technology efforts for the entire organization.

I also recommend that you don't spend too much time stressing over what particular programming language or framework this person specializes in. You need to make sure that they are in possession of good development fundamentals, of course, and that they work in a language that has a decent market following. PHP, Ruby, and Java are each perfectly acceptable languages, and whichever language is used will have a pool of potential hires when the time comes to expand the team.

If you have no technical knowledge whatsoever, then this is the time when you will have to lean hard and often on your board of advisors. Even if you don't personally know someone willing to jump into your venture full-time, you likely know someone who is able to offer meaningful feedback and advice on technical matters. Present your candidates to your advisors along with their code samples and initial thoughts. Advisors with technical knowledge should be able to offer a more advanced perspective on the pool of candidates and be able to make hiring recommendations.

Finally, make sure that this new founder has a restricted stock agreement in place that will require continuous employment for at least a few years. While care should be taken before hiring this person and sinking the time and effort into building the product, you want to have an ironclad escape clause in case there is an unforeseen problem. The last thing you want is to be forced to cut loose a significant equity holder who may reappear down the road demanding compensation. If possible, a contract-to-permanent arrangement might be worth pursuing, which would give you a more simple and straightforward solution to any mis-hire.

Building a new company is fraught with peril, but with a careful approach you should be able to hurdle the first challenge of hiring a technologist with relative ease, and get on with the business of building the product.

QUICK TIPS

1. Incorporate!
2. Business bank account
3. Don't forget about the IRS!
4. Document anything and everything

PAPERWORK

Don't forget the paperwork!

A start-up is an emotional thing.

From the first moment of that initial spark of inspiration, when the world faded to black and all you could see was your unbridled brilliance held forth *(hyperbole: detected)*, you'll undoubtedly be working tirelessly on the mechanics, the motions, of your newfound passion. It is important that you don't get lost in the weeds, so focused on the details, that you forget to create the business!

Business involve paperwork...

...And I repeat: **Don't forget the paperwork!**

The first mess of paper that you need to tackle is incorporation. Incorporating is very important, as it provides you with a lot of liability protection in the unlikely event that your creation accidentally does something unbecoming. Fortunately, incorporation is relatively easy and inexpensive. The simplest, but slightly more expensive option is to use a service, such as LegalZoom or The Company Corporation. These can be very useful aggregation tools if you want to offload a lot of the regulatory and procedural hurdling onto someone else (or if you want to incorporate in another state, such as the state of Delaware). However, you can save a little money by just filing directly. Some states (such as Massachusetts) even offer a basic web application for managing your filing, which makes the process relatively straightforward.

Incorporating will always cost a little money, as each state requires a filing fee of varying amount. Furthermore, the act of incorporating will bring along some iterative costs, such as the filing of your Annual Report. You will also need to identify a registered agent, which is just the person who is responsible for receiving state correspondence (this will usually be yourself). It may seem like a hassle, but if you ever find yourself in a some sort of legal tussle, you'll be happy that your assets are properly shielded from any litigation.

After incorporating, I highly recommend that you open a business bank account. While it isn't necessarily essential, and I am not aware of any law that requires it, it is much safer and proper to avoid any business-related transactions out of a personal account. And since most banks will let you open a business checking account with a very small initial deposit, and credit unions are often clamoring to sign-up local businesses, you really have no excuse. It will all be worth it the first time you need to pay an employee or write a big check to a partner.

The next mess of paperwork that you will need to tackle is your corporate tax return. It is very likely that you will owe nothing for the first few years as you reinvest aggressively and accrue painfully little revenue, but you will need to file nonetheless. Don't delay on this, either; the very last thing you want to deal with while building a fragile new business is the IRS knocking at the door and demanding access to your documents.

Speaking of documents:

Keep a record of everything you do! When the team makes any decision, document that action in meeting minutes. If you use your own money for any business expenses, make sure you keep track of your investment (and always deposit the money into the business bank account first to preserve a proper chain of custody). Anytime the business makes any purchase, be sure that your ledger is up to date. Any contracts, partnerships, agreements, or handshakes made on behalf of the company need to be noted or photocopied and filed away. You should even keep track of phone calls and e-mail. These things may not seem important now, but you will want to form good habits before the company grows; and when the company is entertaining an investment or exit someday, investors and acquiring companies will want to see everything. Diligence is already drawn out and painful, and you don't want to make it any worse with gaps in your record keeping.

Finally, make sure you have proper agreements in place with all founders, advisors, and investors (including your uncle). It may be tempting to work on faith in the early days, and an employment agreement may seem a little too "corporate," but these documents can be essential when there is trouble (and there is almost always some trouble, unfortunately). Carve up the equity collectively, and then codify that division in some restricted stock agreements. Make sure your advisors have their role formalized, and their compensation (if any) well-documented. Be thorough and careful, and then you don't have to worry anymore.

A start-up may be a mission of passion, but a business is built on paperwork. Build the business, do all the paperwork, then indulge your passion!

QUICK TIPS

1. Be smart!
2. Don't be overly protective
3. Accept that dilution is normal and okay
4. No personal debt!

EQUITY AND DEBT

The very most precious thing that an experienced entrepreneur will ever hold is their equity. They will guard that bundle of treasure jealously, fending off many investors, employees, friends, and family like a hungry dog with a bone. At times, they can even be a little *too* aggressive, especially with potential financiers and original team members.

Conversely, the most common mistake of the inexperienced entrepreneur is to be reckless with their equity, using it broadly and often in lieu of salary and benefits for even low-level employees. It has been said that an early indication of a first-time founder will be a cap table with ten or more entries. Inexperience, it seems, can breed carelessness.

You don't want to make either mistake.

Don't be too stingy, nor too loose, with your

equity. Think carefully and intelligently about each grant and the long-term implications it may have on your capital structure. Be ever-conscious that what equity you retain will represent the reward potential of any future liquidity event, and recognize that those who work closely and passionately beside you will want to share some in that reward. Know that investors are going to take a sizable bite of the pie (probably more than you would prefer), so fight hard to retain as much as you can without refusing to make a deal. Consider all avenues for fundraising and compensation, and be creative.

In The Beginning...

The original team of founders, whether it be one or fifteen, should divide the company evenly using restricted stock agreements. Doing so will help to reduce friction and will make decision-making a straightforward vote. Don't worry about creating an option pool at this stage of the game; you are unlikely to be hiring all that much for some time. Equity distribution at this stage will be functionally meaningless except in times of disagreement, but it will set the stage for what is to come (hopefully). And don't forget to declare your equity to the IRS, or else risk a painful tax day down the road.

Friends, Family, and Fools

The earliest investments will usually come from people that you know personally. Unless these first friendly financiers are kicking in a serious amount of money, be sure that you grant them equity in line with their investment amount, and not in line with their personal importance to you. A beloved uncle who invests $5,000, no matter how handsome he may be, should only be getting 1%-3%, not 25% or more. Mistakes made at this level of the game can become serious headaches when the big investments arrive, and a cap table filled with bloated small-time investors can even kill a deal.

Seeding

Your very first professional investment is very likely going to come from an Angel investor (or perhaps several Angels), an Angel group, or a seed fund. These types of investments are often smaller than venture deals and will demand approximately 15%-25% equity depending on the amount invested and how risky the investor believes the company to be. This is also when you will carve out the option pool, as this first infusion of capital will likely be used to grow the team, and start-up aficionados will demand a small slice of the pie.

At this point, you might find yourself starting to worry about your dilution; if you began with two founders with an even split of 50%, you might find yourself now sitting at around 25%-30% (with your uncle and the investors taking the rest). But you shouldn't panic, as this is quite normal. That 25% is worth a lot more than your 50% was worth.

Venture

By the time you attract the attention of a venture capital firm, you'll probably be making some money (or, if you're following an adoption-first approach, a substantial customer base). Venture capital, unlike the first investors and seed funds, is usually serious money. While an Angel investor might be willing to invest $50,000 to $100,000 into a start-up, a venture fund could be willing to invest millions (depending on your business need).

In return for such a substantial sum of cash, a venture firm will be taking the biggest bite of the pie, possibly as high as 45% (or more) depending on your leverage and ability to negotiate. However, you still should not be panicking! Your slice of the equity may now be diluted to only 10%-20%, but the value of that slice is now significantly higher than ever before; in fact, depending on the size of your venture round, you might even find yourself a paper millionaire (which doesn't really mean much, but it's kinda cool nonetheless).

Executives!

After you complete your Series A round, you might discover that your company needs to attract it's first outside executive (perhaps an early-stage CEO or CTO). While the corporate world might be willing to pay exorbitantly for a top-level executive, a venture-backed start-up will need to be just a little more reserved. Therefore, this first executive will likely represent your first significant use of the option pool you made a while back. While the first round of developers, designers, sales professionals, and customer service representatives might have taken a bit, they will only represent a fraction of the whole; but a CEO will command 1%-2% in order to accept such a reduced salary. You will want to make use of your board when negotiating this hire.

Exit and Reward

Assuming all goes as planned, even if you've been subjected to further rounds of venture capital and dilution, you should arrive at your exit point with somewhere between 10% and 20% of the total equity. If this exit happens to be a public offering, you will have to pay substantially for an investment banker to manage the process; however, you may also be realizing a substantial reward. For example, when Facebook went public back in 2012, Mark Zuckerberg was in possession of a 22% ownership stake in the company, valued at $19.1 billion!

Similarly, an acquisition can be very lucrative for founding members; when Google purchased YouTube in 2006 for $1.65 billion, Chad Hurley received an amazing $395 million in compensation. This is when your careful planning will pay off!

I also would like to offer a word of advice on the issue of debt. For those with an overprotective sense of equity, it may be tempting to manage the company through personal debt. However, I will go ahead and strongly discourage you from doing so unless you have *significant* assets. The passion of a start-up may breed visions of invincibility, but I implore you to be pragmatic and recognize that many start-ups fail. You do not want to find your home at risk if the worst materializes.

That being said, *company* debt that is acquired after revenue has started to flow and become predictable can be a valuable tool for protecting equity, promoting growth, and managing operations. As always, consult with a professional.

When done right, equity is responsible for some of the most dramatic and inspiring increases in personal wealth. The dizzying world of the start-up has turned countless men and women of the common classes into millionaires and billionaires seemingly overnight. While there may be more failures than successes, if success arrives you will want to ensure that can share in the great reward. Manage your equity intelligently, and you may find yourself a very happy founder!

QUICK TIPS

1. Incubate for concentrated advice
2. Look for local programs
3. Personalize your application
4. Avoid relocation

INCUBATORS

The start-up is not rare. There are several hundreds of thousands of new businesses in the United States every single year (which complements the hundreds of thousands of businesses that shut down every year). In fact, the Small Business Administration has estimated that there are over 28 million small business in the United States that have at least one employee (and another 22 million self-employment businesses) operating at any given time. That is a staggering number of ventures that are arriving and departing every year, all of which are (or were) vying for the attention and money of the consumer in various markets and locations.

The American economy and consumer class is, thankfully, enormous and able to support many of these ventures; and globalization has further made the potential market for these businesses even larger (you can thank the internet for that). However, it is still a finite market, and it will always be a little bit of a challenge to try and stand out from the crowd and make enough noise.

Enter: **Incubators**.

Business incubators and start-up accelerators are an ever-increasing and popular option for launching a new venture. In 2006, there were 1,100 business incubators operating in only North America, and they graduated an amazing 27,000 businesses that generated $17B in single-year revenue. Today, even in spite of the economic downturn of 2008, there are now 1,400 incubators operating and they expect to graduate just shy of 50,000 ventures this year!

The model for a business incubator is relatively well established (although each incubator usually puts a bit of spin at the edges of the archetype for the sake of variety and attraction). They usually have an admissions period, followed by a rigorous selection process and the start of an education and implementation program.

During that program, founders are given access to an intense growth promotion process, which often one-on-one mentorship, and are usually given access to office space and facilities. Sometimes they are given small sums of operating capital. At the end of the program, a "winner" is often chosen and given a substantial monetary reward (or investment) and free press attention and promotion.

These incubator programs are often non-profit,

driven by local economic development efforts and the philanthropic desires for local growth, and they are powered through donation (and occasionally equity grants). The programs have become wildly popular in political and charitable circles because they have an astonishing success rate, with 87% of graduating companies remaining in operation five years after the date of graduation.

If you should have the opportunity to participate in an incubation program, I highly recommend that you do. The guidance and experience, and operating capital, can be invaluable when you're launching a new venture, and there is no more concentrated and dedicated source of either. Most programs do not have an application fee, so you can happily apply to as many as you wish; however, be sure that the program you are applying to is somewhat relevant to your business model and industry, and tailor your application to the criteria of each program. The industry is vast, but everyone still talks to everyone else, and any venture that spam-applies to every program will get noticed and discussed. Be genuine and do your research.

While there are several virtual incubators, and most incubators will accept a non-local applicant, I highly recommend that you target programs in your geographic area. I don't recommend relocation for any program that doesn't come coupled with some guaranteed operating capital. There are incubators all over the country (and world), and you're almost certain to find one local to you. For example, in the city of Boston there are 10 incubators operating in just the metro area, and they graduate just under 250 ventures every year (this includes the world-famous TechStars and MassChallenge).

Do some research, tighten up your pitch deck and executive summary, and find a program that will best help you succeed. If you give the program the proper respect and time, it can be the difference between success and failure.

QUICK TIPS

1. It doesn't have to be perfect!
2. Get something in front of the people!
3. Expect criticism, flaws, and complaints
4. Move fast, think fast

THE MVP

So, you have a great idea...

...that's awesome! Now you have to identify the market opportunity and craft your business plan, recruit an early team (likely out of your friends and colleagues), and start to plan your strategy. As you work furiously, a time will come quickly when you need to develop the minimum viable version of your product. You will need to put something in front of your early adopters and trusted advisors to solicit for feedback and criticism.

You start to develop, beginning with nothing, weaving your great idea into existence! Before you know it, that idea will be usable (somewhat); you can register new accounts and login, see the basic features, and have a rough understanding of what is the business brand. It's not going to be perfect by any means, but it will be coming together and will be functionally usable.

The critical question arises:

When is it ready for release?

One of the most common (and most dangerous) mistakes in the entrepreneurial world is to wait for product perfection. Founders develop a maniacal focus on improvements, feature creation, process smoothing; they want to release a product that shines from day one!

Unfortunately, all the delays from the pursuit of perfection can often cripple or destroy the chance of success. The technology market moves very fast, faster than most realize, and no matter how unique you think your idea is or what kind of market it is now in, I promise you that others are working on something similar. It is not essential that you be the first to market, but you do need to be in the market as fast as possible. You need early customers, you need criticism, and you need the time and space to make changes and improve your vision before the harsh spotlights of the media are on you in force.

You need time to fail!

So, again, the question is: **When?**

Before you begin to develop, it is important that you identify the core features of your vision. What *must* the product have for it to be considered at all functional? For example, if you were setting out to build a beautiful throne as quickly as possible, released in stages (in keeping with Agile principles), the first step would be to create a basic chair: four legs, a seating surface, and back support. It should not be missing anything important, it should be recognizable as a chair, but it should also have little extras beyond a coat of paint.

That simple creation would not be the final product, of course; there is still a long way to go and much more to do. But it's enough to begin testing, and will provide you with a platform for further development. Once you get some assurances that the minimum viable product is of quality and worth pursuing further, then you can begin adding the bells and whistles that will become the throne.

So, you have your chair and you release...

...what happens next?

One of the primary reasons why the tendency toward a maniacal focus on pre-release perfection is foolish is that most products will be released with little fanfare. Unless you are an established presence and have some media clout, your product will find only a handful of search-sourced users in the first few days. It's during this lull in activity that you should be actively recruiting and encouraging early adopters, either out of your own network of trusted colleagues or the limited search traffic.

This crew of early-adopters should be able to provide you with the feedback and criticism that is often impossible to generate in the echo chamber of the office. You shouldn't take every comment as gospel, of course, and don't order any immediate and panic-driven changes, but you should still pay attention to trends and be cognizant of genuine complaints (bugs, missing important features, bad experience and process, etc).

I recommend at least a single effort at revision and repair before beginning any serious marketing and media efforts. Make sure the MVP will hold up well to general pressure. That being said, you still must put some strain on your creation long before the throne is fully complete. Don't turn away any willing users. Put as many eyes as possible on your vision and get ready to think, develop, and speak rapidly and with clarity, and make changes were necessary. The early days of a venture are chaotic, thrilling, perilous, crazy, and fun, and only a certain personality is well-suited for such an adventure. If you have it within you to go down this road, I wish you nothing but success!

QUICK TIPS

1. Poor design is unacceptable today
2. Brand strategy before public exposure
3. KISS
4. Consistency at all times

DESIGN,
FORGET IT NOT!

In the early days of the web, when the dot-com bust was still a few years away and the start-up market was gathering steam, there existed a truly abysmal standard of usability and design. I can remember companies that attracted several million dollars in venture capital, and even companies that would go public, that boasted website designs that could today be architected by a seizing toddler.

In the interest of fairness, it is worth mentioning that alot of this visual horror was not really the fault of the offending companies; rather, it was the fault of the capabilities of the browser and the average connection speeds of the home. The standard today has been greatly elevated. Poor design is no longer acceptable. Usability is now paramount for success.

Consumers have developed a very low tolerance for a difficult experience, and they'll make displeasure known, loudly. If you want to be able to succeed, no matter what market you are serving, you need to invest (at least a little) in design and experience.

I should make it clear that I'm not saying you should make an immediate design spend. In the first days of a start-up, you can safely operate a cludgy website so long as it has some basic usability. That first iteration won't be getting much attention from the outside world, and you can carefully attract a core of early adopters that will understand what "minimum viable" means. You'll be making a lot of changes to that first attempt, almost every day, as you build your feature set, and your focus has to be on functionality (just make it work). As the service becomes more popular, however, and your user base continues to expand, you are going to have to invest in a strong second design. The more eyes that are on your first rough cut, the higher the risk of a public spread of negative reviews.

Ideally you want someone on your founding team that is capable of managing this first revision (for free). But if no such design talent is present, you can leverage existing online talent networks to find someone willing to work on the cheap (or for delayed comp or equity); AngelList and LinkedIn are excellent resources for this kind of search. Technical conferences and professional meetups are also good resources. You will want to target young designers and recent college graduates who are looking to build the first entries of a portfolio.

Don't expect a world-class result from this first inexpensive effort with an inexperienced resource, but it will be better than what you have and will be an important first step forward. It will ready your business for the safe attraction of a wider audience.

You will need to work closely with this the design resource for this first design overhaul, and there are a few principles you should keep in mind. Most importantly, adhere to the KISS principle as often as possible (Keep It Simple, Stupid). With every new page, paragraph, heading, image, and feature, be on the lookout for potential cuts and reductions. Design studies have consistently proven that consumers prefer products that are simple and straightforward, and a clean, uncluttered interface is inherently pleasing to the human eye. Unless your product specifically targets a niche that favors pomp and circumstance (such as sports or entertainment), I recommend keeping colors muted and soft. Use text sparingly; say much with little. You don't need to add any long, expository paragraphs to convince the consumer to participate (because they won't be reading them, anyway).

Keep your fonts and colors consistent.

One of the first visual markers of a bad design are mismatched fonts, colors and images. A website is a single product, and it should look like it. And don't go overboard on the flashy options (video backgrounds, parallax scrolling, fading and swiping images, etc). A little flash goes a long way, and too much makes a site look overly busy and desperate. You will want to convey a sense of confidence and casual elegance. And make certain whatever design principles and brand patterns you eventually choose are consistent across all materials, from letters to pens. If you decide to revise your brand, incorporate those revisions in all materials at the same time; don't use a different logo on your letterhead than on your homepage. The observer should always know immediately what company they are observing.

A good design and user experience is crucial in the modern landscape, and can be tremendously lucrative when done excellently. Consumers like products that fit with their sensibilities, and will pay for it; Apple has become one of the world's most profitable companies by taking existing technology and redesigning it with an emphasis on the user experience. You want to be like Apple and take design seriously! The best algorithms in the world will be bested by a business that builds for their consumer, and not their intellectual ego.

QUICK TIPS

1. Work smart, not endlessly
2. The work will never end, so take breaks
3. Learn to disengage and disconnect
4. Take a vacation!

HARD WORK

Have you ever gone on a leisurely late-night walk through the downtown or innovation district of a city during the week, perhaps after a dinner with friends or family? Well, the next time that you do, take a look at the buildings around you and see if you can count the number of offices that are still brightly lit and filled with people; I will bet good money that you can find at least a handful.

And amongst those offices filled with dedicated workers, I am certain that at least a few of them are occupied by start-up teams burning the candle at both ends. The lifeless, eternally-working founder is practically a cliché these days, and it has somehow embedded itself into the fabric of what it means to be an entrepreneur. I have myself met so many men and women from the entrepreneurial world who believe, deep within their souls, that if they are not at the office then they are somehow falling behind.

Well, I am here to shout from whatever hilltop I have available to me, at the top of my lung until my voice is hoarse: **Stop it!**

First of all, working excessively is simply not good business. No matter how productive you may *think* you are, studies have proven irrefutably that excessive work and physical exhaustion will lead to a lowered volume, and a reduced quality, of work. That sensation of achievement you are getting after a long day at the office is a psychological trick; had you worked smarter and more efficiently, you could have accomplished the same amount of work in a fraction of the time. This is especially true in the knowledge-based professions, such as in software engineering, as mistakes that are caused by fatigue can often become exponentially more costly and systemic, and will eventually induce an overall-negative productivity output.

I am not saying that the occasional stretch of extended effort can't reap some short-term reward, but it has to be occasional and measured. Reserve those late-nights and early-mornings for deadlines and serious problems, and put some meaningful boundaries around the rest of your days.

And don't forget: Life is more than just work.

Take it from someone (me) who really, *really* enjoys his work: once in a while, you need to step away and recharge, or you'll burn out and learn to hate the office. There are books that need to be read, sights that need to be seen, family that needs to be enjoyed, and friends that need to be met.

Also, let's not lose sight of the fact that the sun is an important component in producing Vitamin D, and a long-term deficiency in Vitamin D can lead to depression, cardiovascular disease, and cancer. So protect your health and get outside once in a while!

Now, the critical question: *How?*

Founders don't work really hard for the sake of working; you won't find a founder at his desk past midnight twiddling his thumbs and waiting for the sun to rise, loving every minute of the harsh lighting and bitter coffee. Rather, a founder will overwork themselves because they truly believe that they have to; they see a mountain of work before them and no time in which to do it all, so they try to solve the problem with shear force of will.

The first step in tackling this belief is to admit that it is actually a lie. You are busy, yes, that much is true. But you will *always* be busy. Forever.

It's never going away, there is no finish line to cross, there is no final exam to take. Humongous corporations with multi-billion-dollar budgets and decades of history are still very busy and working hard. You need to learn to accept that some things will not get done today; some things will get done tomorrow, or next week, or next month, or never. Learn to prioritize your task list, to focus on what is truly most important, and then assign yourself firm deadlines and a strict schedule. In fact, unless there is a genuine crisis or a critical need (and be honest with yourself, because no one is going to do it for you), then I recommend that you arrive at the office and leave for the night at the same time every day. I would target about 7-9 hours in office, depending on your individual temperament and productivity.

And when you do go home, *go home!*

At whatever hour you decide to leave the office, stop working. Sitting on the couch and answering e-mails, writing code, and reviewing reports is not relaxing. You have to learn to disengage. Too many entrepreneurs have a persistent and often paralyzing fear that if they stop thinking about work for too long, they will somehow lose their place and fall behind. Well, I am here to promise you that you won't fall behind. When you return to the office in the morning, you will remember exactly where you left off, and you will jump right back into the thick of things and kick some ass.

Spend your time out of the office with family and friends, watching some television, or reading leisurely; go to the beach, go camping, whatever, just stay away from work and stay off your phone. You will be amazed at how refreshed and ready to conquer you will feel in the morning.

Furthermore, take a genuine vacation every now and then. This is especially important once you've passed the earliest phases of a new venture and have started building a team. If you can't trust your employees to run the show for a few days, then you should probably be looking for new employees.

Excess and overwork are a few start-up clichés that really have to die; hard work is an integral part of success, but there is a right way and a wrong way to work hard, and refusing to enjoy your life is the wrong way. Find a balance and you'll find that everything, including work, gets a little better.

QUICK TIPS

1. Find three trusted advisors
2. Network like a politician
3. Compensate advisors appropriately
4. Nurture relationships and ask for advice

ADVISORS

One of the most important and difficult early moves for a new start-up is to secure some quality advisors to help shape the growth and strategy of the effort. Unless you are a seasoned serial entrepreneur with a few successful exits under your belt, you will likely need some significant guidance as you navigate the dangerous waters of the entrepreneurial world.

While an advisor certainly can't guarantee any amount of success, a good stable of mentors can be a vital calm amidst the roiling storm. And they can be critical to raising funds, too!

- But where do you find these advisors?

- How do you ask them for help?

- How much can you expect them to give?

- How often should you connect with them?

- Should you compensate them?

- What should they be doing, exactly?

Those who've previously been a mere employee in a start-up effort (or in the corporate world, for that matter) may already have developed a network of people worth soliciting for advice (and these trusted sources are certainly the best recruits). But for those of you who are at the very beginning, the best method for securing a good stable of advisors is to network like your very life depended on it (and frankly, this is good advice for anyone in any field).

Attend meet-ups and lectures and conferences, and talk candidly with everyone you meet; ask for referrals, ask for advice, and always be polite and responsive. Professional organizations can also be a great starting point. MassTLC, for example, hosts some excellent events (such as the now famous unConference) that attract some exceptional talent. Ask for business cards, phone numbers, and e-mail addresses; and follow up immediately.

Be proactive!

Once you've started to develop your network, take some time to identify those who seem to have an understanding of good entrepreneurial practices, and also care enough to share. Seek out people who have built their own businesses, currently own their own business, and/or have had a successful exit.

Look for those who've played the game more than once, and try to find someone in a similar industry (without being a direct competitor).

Create a list of your five favorite candidates and begin a dialogue with each separately. Ask for some detailed advice and feedback, be friendly, and begin to nurture the budding relationship. Recruiting an advisor from a fresh network is a little like dating: you have to flirt a little before you can ask them out for coffee, and then you need a few coffee dates before you can invite them into your house for dinner. You want to be genuine; even if you don't find an advisor, you will surely be finding someone worth knowing. And if they do seem like a fit, when you feel comfortable, approach them with the idea of formal advisorship.

A formal advisor is someone worth promoting. You want to be able to point to that person's name in a pitch deck or business plan and say to complete strangers, "that person believes in my business, and they are helping it grow," and that statement should mean something. The advisor is someone you will be mentioning to clients, investors, and potential partners. They should have some real value to offer the business, both direct and emotional. And with that intrinsic value, an advisor is someone worth compensating, even if only very slightly; not with money, of course, but rather with a dash of equity.

As many will have told you by now, including myself (and rightly so), you must be guarded and careful with your equity; but you also need to be willing to use just a little (just the right amount) to entice others to really care about, and work toward, your success. There is no perfect amount of equity to offer to an advisor, so use your best judgment. A good starting point is around a fraction of a percent (perhaps 0.25%). Offer it as part of your formal request for advisorship, and sell the value.

I will recommend settling on a rather small but formidable board of advisors. Don't go overboard - three advisors should be sufficient. Each advisor should bring a little something different to the table. If you are building a web-based sales business, for example, I recommend having a technical advisor, an executive advisor, and a sales advisor. This will give you the means of getting helpful guidance in all many of the challenges you are about to face without bombarding one individual with an endless stream of questions and concerns.

You should connect with each advisor regularly, but not obsessively. I will suggest between 2 and 4 meetings per month. If possible, get the advisors talking to each other; you could hold a conference call once in a while and get everyone together at the same time. Have the whole team meet at least once per quarter, preferably in person. Use this time of gathering to discuss ongoing business development and strategy, recent successes, and upcoming needs. Ask your advisors for referrals, to review materials, and to make recommendations. Practice your pitch. Leverage the experience they offer and let them help you build a business. Don't do everything they recommend, of course, but be engaged and listen closely. They are there for a reason.

A good advisor certainly won't guarantee your success, but they will usually be able to help bring success just a little closer to your reach. And at the very least, they are likely to become a part of your professional circle for many years to come, so be a good friend and colleague and help each other reach success. You'll be thankful for them in the end.

QUICK TIPS

1. Version one can be rough...
   ...but version two cannot.
2. Review after capital
3. Involve your advisors
4. Don't go overboard, think smart

ARCHITECTING

As a technology start-up begins to grow and scale, one of the most common pain points will be finding the right balance between speed to deployment and architecting for the future.

The first product out of the door is usually (and probably should be) a little clunky. You don't want to waste any time and energy working in a feedback vacuum, and as I've mentioned before the pursuit of pre-release perfection can be a recipe for disaster. There are some narrow exceptions, but it is almost always better to release fast and early.

You have to publish!

Publish or perish, as they say...

It is critical that you get something in front of the people. You need precious feedback. The world is teeming with failed ventures that spent months and years in development hell trying to get the first version to perfection. You want to fail fast, to take criticism in stride, and retool where needed quickly and efficiently. You should, of course, invest enough in time and thought to avoid needing a complete rewrite at any point in the near future (taking care of the basics, building a good foundation, because the fundamentals of good development haven't changed all that much), but don't be too picky.

But also know that eventually, as you grow and advance, you will become just a little bit picky.

The issue is *when*.

As traction builds, the minimum viable product that was pushed out the door will likely become somewhat unreliable. It will last a good long while if it was built well enough, of course, but even the strongest first attempts will almost always start to fall over during times of extreme stress, and the glut of feature requests, bug reports, and other needs will quickly grow out of control.

The single server that you hosted in the cloud at the cheapest rate while bootstrapping will no longer handle your needs; the embedded services that were created and edited quickly and sloppily will make scaling webheads more complex and error prone, and you'll need a better data architecture to handle the load. The slurry of commentless, sloppy code will become exposed to more developers, many of them junior, and you won't have time to carefully assist and educate each of them. Eventually you will need to take a breath, step back, and evaluate what measures you need to implement to prepare for serious long-term growth.

And ideally you'll do this before you *have* to.

In my experience, the most painful mistake is to wait just a little too long before considering and architecting for the future. The management team will sometimes cling to the launch product and try to ride it to the finish line, but it will always get too tired and collapse before the end. And when market forces force you to consider retooling, the pressures on yourself, your team, and your system will be immense and difficult to manage.

I'm sure that every developer worth mentioning has at least one memory of an overnight marathon triage session, trying desperately to engineer on the fly a system that can handle a large client or sudden arrival of users that they weren't properly prepared for. While some may argue that such moments are just the hallmarks of a start-up, the circumstances are almost always avoidable with just a little bit of planning and forethought.

I can't offer any sweeping generalized guidance; every start-up is a little different. But somewhere after the first moneyed event (whether it be an investment round or securing the first paying client) you should consider that your system might be in need of a review. Don't over-think this, of course, and don't go overboard. You certainly don't need to hire independent auditors or dedicate your entire technical staff to an internal review. You are still a start-up and should act like a start-up. But you should start to think a little bit faster than the moment. Have your senior person (the technical lead, the early-stage CTO, or a trusted advisor) take a look at your setup, document your configurations, and consider what might be necessary at certain milestones. Such information can be invaluable as you plan for new clients, press releases, and product announcements; you'll know which way the wind is blowing and you'll be able to take proactive steps before the tornado arrives.

QUICK TIPS

1. Think cheap!
2. Fully leverage your team
3. Cut corners and go free wherever possible
4. Look, talk, and think big

BOOTSTRAPPING

Large open spaces that sit at the top of towering skyscrapers with floor-to-ceiling windows; elegant paintings above avant-garde desks, chairs, and zany layouts; free-flowing wine and beer; free MacBook Pros and raging parties set in Las Vegas; SUV's and ping-pong, and Xbox...

The media (and the late 90's) have exaggerated and glamorized the start-up venture to the point of absurdity, focusing only on the largest and the most grandiose imagery from a broad, diverse and non-contiguous industry. The sad reality for the vast majority of start-ups, even the very successful ones, is that for much of their existence they will function on very little (or no) money. There will not be any free Apple products or the renting of prime office space near the waterfront. They won't be giving out unlimited free food or access to a company car. There will be no wild parties in Vegas, and their desks will probably be made of plastic.

To succeed, the best entrepreneurs will learn the virtue of running a business on fumes and forcing it to succeed anyway. We call this **bootstrapping**.

The most abundant resource in the bootstrapped company is the labor, passion, and intelligence of the founding team, who are often willing to work for pennies (or nothing) for several years in search of greatness. Companies that outsource their early work to contractors and consultants will likely find themselves uncomfortably tight on funds later on down the road (or worse, in possession of a painful cap table). This is why it is so important to build a well-rounded and exceptional founding team that has the ambition and capacity to really build a new venture. At least one of the founding core should have some business experience (or education), and at least one should have some technical expertise (or education). You should be able to build the MVP as a group without dipping into your limited funds.

Beyond the team, the most important aspect of bootstrapping involves finding ways to cut corners without sacrificing company growth or opportunity. For instance, you should not be renting any office space at the very beginning; work out of someone's home, or your own garage. Rent a virtual office in order to receive mail and to apply for bank accounts and other services. If you need to host an in-person meeting with a client or investor, there are a number of places where you can rent a conference room relatively cheaply (for example, Regus has offices and conference rooms for rent in many major cities around the world). Get business cards and stationary from VistaPrint or another inexpensive on-demand printing service, and use a cellphone for business calls (or an online centralized service, like Google Voice). Use open-source office software suites, like LibreOffice or OpenOffice, and setup your e-mail on a free (or very cheap) hosted solution (almost all domain registrars offer cheap or free options). And if you need to get it, consider only inexpensive but respected SSL certificates (you can get them for as cheap as $10/year from some providers).

Never pay someone to write a business plan!

More on that later...

For internet-based companies, use the cheapest available options while getting everything started. Amazon Web Services, for example, sells products with a very wide expense profile, and many include a very cheap (or even nearly free) option for low-bandwidth services. A few micro instances on EC2 and you can have a load-balanced system, with a proper master-slave database configuration, for less than $50/month. Make sure all active development is done with open-source languages, and only use open-source plugins and packages wherever it is possible; Ubuntu Server running PHP or Ruby, with MySQL or Mongo, serving a frontend that uses a standard JavaScript library, like jQuery or Angular will get you an excellent product with no expense. Use your personal computer for everything, and if you don't have a printer you can print on the cheap at your local library.

Learn how to market and promote your products without spending on advertisements, press releases, or sponsored campaigns. Leverage social media to the fullest extent possible, be engaged and active in your community, and develop a relationship with a few reporters and industry professionals. If you do feel compelled to send a press release, write the copy on your company blog and then use a free distribution service to get the content in front of aggregation services. You can find a lot of important media contacts with a simple Google search (or by targeting the publications of your choosing).

Learn the art of looking bigger than you actually are. None of your clients, partners, potential investors, or media contacts need to know that you primarily work out of your home, or that you're using your cellphone as a business phone, or that you are manually tweeting all of those updates. Talk in the plural when appropriate ("we" always sounds better than "I") and be vague with your team size and authority. You would be amazed at how many companies have been adept at "faking" scale; there was once a time when Google was being hosted out of a Stanford dorm room, and was operating for a few years before they even incorporated!

Bootstrapping can be quite a stressful, terrible endeavor, but it can be the difference between success and failure in the long run. Don't be afraid to walk the tightrope; you will be in good company, and you will be grateful when you've made it and the business finally starts to grow.

QUICK TIPS

1. Probably won't happen...
2. Get a warm introduction!
3. Have a defensible revenue model
4. Focus on product development

FUNDRAISING

It took me a good long while to decide whether or not to talk about this; there are already a thousand-million books, articles, lectures, and blogs in every conceivable medium and format that discuss the issue of start-up fundraising, and not one has been able to offer up any remarkable new insights not yet covered extensively by others (and this will be no exception, truthfully). That being said, the number one question that I still hear all the time from every entrepreneur is: "How am I able to raise money for my business?" It would seem that no matter how often and aggressively this topic is covered, there are always a sizable number of people who don't know the basics. Thus, it is with a heavy heart and a sense of nostalgia that I write today about how to (maybe, possibly) secure financing for your venture.

First, and most importantly:

Don't get too excited (just yet).

I'm sure, just like everyone else, you have heard of at least one of the thousands of success stories that have been swirling around the news over the last decade. It usually involves a plucky college student who secures hundreds of millions of dollars in venture capital, and then gets acquired by Google a few years later for a few billion.

It is a thrilling and captivating story, and it does occasionally happen under special circumstances, but it is extremely rare and very unlikely to ever happen to you; there is a reason why these stories are so noteworthy and interesting. The vast majority of private investment is smaller, and they happen to far fewer companies than you might think.

There are 462 venture capital firms active in the United States as of 2012 (the vast majority of which reside in California, Massachusetts, New York, or Texas), and in 2012 they made investments in just 3,698 companies. With $26.5B in provided funding that year, that amounts to an average of $7.17M per company; however, this figure is somewhat skewed by the presence of a handful of mega-transactions in middle-market companies. When we consider only start-up businesses, there were only 67 seed-stage venture investments in the last quarter of 2012, and those averaged $2.3M per company.

These numbers may still seem impressive until you consider that there are approximately 1,100 business incubators in operation today in North America; in 2011 alone, these incubators graduated a truly staggering number of quality ventures (over 49,000)! The paltry 3,698 companies that received venture funding in 2012 only scratched the surface of the total number of companies that likely sought financing, the majority of which would have been denied. Angels, institutional investors, and other alternative financing methods fill some of the gap, but the reality is that a large number of companies, some of which may even be deserving, will never see serious outside financial support.

What does this mean?

It means that you must make sure that you have a business model that doesn't *depend* on outside financing to succeed. Angel and venture investment should be seen as a means to accelerating existing growth and to prepare for broad expansion, not as a catalyst for getting up off the ground. And not quite so surprisingly, having such a business model will be the first of many factors in promoting your company to those potential investors; these men and women want to see sustainable business models with a defined and clear path to success.

Okay, now that we have that out of the way...

One of the most important aspects of securing capital is the **warm introduction**. The financial industry is a remarkably small community, and they all like to talk (a lot); it's a big party, and gossip is the currency of the realm. It may seem a little snooty, but I can assure you it is not. The reality, both statistically and anecdotally, is that a warm introduction generates a substantially higher chance of overall success than a cold one. Investors may have more money than you do, but those coffers are not unlimited, and they need to be judicious when selecting potential opportunities. When a trusted member of their network is willing to personally vouch for the quality of the founding team at a particular venture, that acts as the first piece of unofficial due diligence.

How do you secure a warm introduction?

Honestly, there isn't a single answer. Sometimes a family member can be the gateway (does your uncle work in the finance space? Maybe he knows someone); at other times, it'll be a prior professional connection. Your board of advisors will be willing to assist (as I have discussed previously), and it is not a bad idea to find business partners with large rolodexes that they're willing to share. Ultimately, however, the best connections will develop through organic networking; you want to go to events and talk about your business. Shake hands with people and exchange business cards; get to know the important players in your space and around your neighborhood. Don't be pushy, and don't demand any help (no one likes to feel like they are being taken advantage of or pushed around), but always be ready to talk about your idea and always accept an invitation to connect.

Once you get yourself a warm introduction, make sure that you make the best of it by ensuring that your materials are refined. No one expects a polished prospectus from an early-stage start-up, but make sure you've fleshed out the nitty-gritty of your financial model and how you'll make money (know when you intend to break-even and what it will cost to get there); make sure you've done your market research and are able to defend your value proposition; have your cap table developed and keep it clean; know your weaknesses and have a plan for fixing them; and have something real and tangible to show! Investors hear a lot of pitches, and they will have no patience for a team with only a PowerPoint and a couple of documents. Build your MVP, get some initial customers, get some early feedback, and start developing a viable community. Investors want serious opportunities, and a pattern of growth within a real product is the quickest way to demonstrate that opportunity.

Finally, never focus all of your energy on fundraising. There is always a strong temptation to do so, but remember that your product has to be the priority. You may never get that investment and you should be able to succeed (albeit more slowly) without it. And even if you do manage to secure an investment, those investors will want to see a team that is engaged and committed to success. A vibrant and evolving product that has no development gaps due to fundraising efforts is the best way to promote yourself to those interested parties and keep your investors happy and relaxed.

QUICK TIPS

1. Never pay for a business plan or deck!
2. Focus on executive summary and financials
3. Capture the attention of the audience
4. Focus on the product

PLANS AND PITCHES

One of the most unfortunate and uncomfortable stories that I've ever heard in my entrepreneurial conversations came from from a young founder out of the midwest. Strapped for cash but ambitious and motivated, this would-be entrepreneur paid nearly $5,000 to have a "professionally designed" business plan created for them. This founder believed such an expense would be critical to fundraising, and that they would be unable to complete the "required" and "complicated" work themselves. I almost felt like a brute as I explained that this was a completely unnecessary expense, that business plan creation services are essentially scams designed to prey on the passions of young and inexperienced business owners, and that they absolutely could have done all the work themselves with no problems. In order to hopefully help others avoid such a mistake, I will give this summation it's own paragraph:

Never pay for a business plan or pitch deck!

I promise, from the bottom of my heart, that you can create both of these documents yourself without too much anguish (and you may not even need the business plan at all). First of all, there already exists a pretty good free wizard for creating a business plan, offered by the Small Business Administration. The SBA also provides a lot of instructional and educational materials around starting a business, structuring your business, and raising funds. They are a dangerously underutilized resource that can save many entrepreneurs a lot of time, money, and heartache, and they are anxious to help.

But, as I has just mentioned, you probably don't even need to write a complete business plan at all; investors rarely require more than an executive summary, financial documents, and a pitch deck prior to a formal due diligence process. The most value that a business plan could offer is to the founder themselves, acting as a sort of "blue print" for a previously envisioned business execution. In the mayhem of a start-up, it can be easy to sidetrack yourself, and a business plan may act as a compass in tough times. But an internal document does not require tremendous pain or expense to generate.

For investors and any potential partners, focus largely on the executive summary. This document will be short, often 1-3 pages in total, and will not offer significant detail; as it's name implies, this is a summary only. You will give a brief explanation of the business, what you've accomplished so far and what your immediate goals are, and explain the core problem that you're trying to solve. You'll put some numbers around the size of your target market. This document should be written with a little bit of panache, but only insofar as it does not detract from the message; be attractive, but don't be distracting.

After the summary is complete, you will want to put some insight around your financial assumptions. How much money are you looking to raise and how will it be spent; what are your primary expenses, and what is your revenue projection and path to profitability. Be a little optimistic, since any good investor is going to slash your estimates anyway, but don't be unrealistically optimistic (it will make you look inexperienced); and especially don't be pessimistic! You're in this business for a reason, and if you exude an assumption of failure from the start then no one is going to be interested in helping you.

Beyond the summary and finances, the next most important tool for recruiting investors and partners will be the pitch deck. As much as it pains me to confess this, most people will not spend a lot of time thinking about you and your business at all. Investors, for example, likely see thousands of opportunities every year and will be investing in only a handful (possibly less than a dozen). They need to be judicious with their time, and you have to capture the attention of your audience quickly and exceptionally. Unfortunately, such a level of attention is very difficult to achieve in a long-form document. The pitch deck the solution; it is a simple

PowerPoint document (or Google Presentation) that is designed to dazzle. It should be dressed up and ready for showcase; there should be illustrations and easily consumable vehicles for conveying your information. You want the audience to know what you are going to say before you even say it just by looking at the current slide.

The best pitch decks are relatively short, but more detailed than an executive summary. I prefer to keep a presentation at 10 slides or under, but every business model is different, and you don't want to leave any important detail out of the presentation in order to conform to an arbitrary limit. But make sure you are putting emphasis on succinct explanation; don't be verbose! In your revisions, try to find ways to tighten the message and reduce the noise. The more quickly you can get your point across, the more efficiently you will be able to capture and hold attention.

Finally, don't spend too much time planning and documenting. Building a start-up is very difficult, and time is always of the essence; having a vision and a strategy is important, but don't let planning consume you. Spend a few days putting your thoughts to paper, refining your messaging, and then get back to work. If an investor presentation is scheduled, you can come back to your materials and spend a day or two prior on further revisions and tightening, but until then focus on the work. As the old saying goes, "if you spend too much time thinking about a thing, you'll never get it done."

QUICK TIPS

1. Hire carefully and respectfully
2. Don't worry about degrees and extras
3. Make coders write code!
4. Be judicious and open-minded

HIRING

I truly believe, from the very depths of my soul, that one of the most important things that any founder or manager will be doing in a technology business is to hire, and hire well, a solid core of engineers. A team that's composed of motivated, complimentary talent is a team that will produce efficiently and consistently, and require minimal guidance. I have personally observed a great deal of (easily preventable) turnover and pain that resulted only from poor hiring practices, and it saddens me. A poor hire is one of the few acts of management that is universally bad at every level; it's bad for the employee, bad for the manager, bad for the company and bad for the product. No one is happy when an employer does a poor job evaluating a candidate, and so it must be given the greatest focus. And if your start-up ever realizes success, you will absolutely be hiring eventually.

While a lot of this advice is specific to hiring technologists (which is my expertise), I believe that a lot of this is somewhat transferable to other roles.

Part of the usual problem is that no one really knows how to best evaluate a technical candidate (not even the technologists themselves). Everyone thinks that they have the best approach, but when put to the fire almost everyone defaults to the same unreliable and inconsistent methods that have been used for decades. The most common pitfalls of the technical interview are:

1. Focusing on memorization.
2. Not letting the candidate do the talking.
3. Requiring a college degree, certification or fancy internship for consideration.
4. Having poor conversational skills.
5. Falling in love / out of love too fast.

Fortunately, each of these problems is easily solved!

The most important thing you need to do is stop focusing on memory-dependent questions. If a question is easily answered with a quick Google search, then it is a wrong question. It is an industry rule that no technologist should be willing to waste precious brain space memorizing every little tidbit about any specific technology. We have the internet nowadays, and it is remarkably good at helping us solve common problems in no time at all. A good technologist is not made by how many different regular expressions or definitions they happen to have memorized; rather, a good technologist is made by having a well-developed ability to think critically and logically and quickly.

And I should continue here by saying that logic puzzles and word problems are not the solution, either! It became fashionable in the last few years to substitute technical questions for New York Times styled brain teasers (such as "How many golf balls would fit inside an airplane"). These questions are practically useless; a good engineer wouldn't waste time conceptualizing the issue, but would design a program that fills a mock airplane with golf balls and maintains an accurate count!

The second most important thing you need to do in order to hire well is stop worrying about college degrees. This also applies to technical certifications, that Google internship, or any other flashy resume tidbit that is designed to make you say "wow.". Why, you ask? Because such trophies are often, in practice, terrible indicators of success.

Some of the most talented and well respected technologists I've ever worked with never finished college (and some didn't even bother starting), while some of the worst I've ever worked with have had advanced degrees and a sterling resume a mile long. The ability to study diligently and prepare for tests might demonstrate good organizational skills, but it is not an incubator for successful engineering. Software development is all about thinking logically and creatively, responding to adversity with mettle and gumption, and finding pragmatic ways to solve non-obvious problems, and those skills are learned in the fires, not in the classroom.

Is education important?

Of course!

And if you give me two candidates of near equal practical talent and good personality, the educated candidate will get my selection. But it isn't the most important thing, and it gets far too much focus. Even at Google, the tech giant with an infamous penchant for academics, has recently recanted their entire hiring philosophy. The evidence is clear and becoming increasingly obvious to a larger number of companies: education, while valuable, is not the best marker for employment success.

So, given the above, what should you do?

The first thing you need to do is hone your conversational skills. Learn to be friendly and inviting. Don't dominate the conversation, of course, and don't let the candidate rule the meeting, either. Make the individual comfortable, be open, and get them to spill their guts. Get to know their technical background, how they got into technology, how they learned their skills, the companies they've worked for and why they left; ask about past projects and what they're most proud of, and what they are working on now, and what difficult problem was most fun to solve. Learn what technologies they like to work with and why; find out what is their favorite baseball team. What do they do for fun at the end of the day? Get to know the candidate as thoroughly as you possibly can, both professionally and personally, and take diligent notes. That is the only way you can expect to make reasonable assumptions about how best their skills and personality might fit with your team.

The second thing you need to do is make the candidate **write some code**. And don't waste time with a stupid recursive loop function taken from a 1994 textbook that anyone could do in five minutes with half a brain; make them *really* code. Give them some minor, but very real, problem and ask them to solve it. Keep instruction to a minimum and let them do their thing (while aware that they can ask questions freely). Give them some time away from the interview to complete it (consider paying them a small contract fee) and scrutinize the result. You can learn an awful lot about a programmer just from reading a little original code.

Finally, don't be afraid to let a candidate go. I don't care how amazing a resume may seem, or how great of a talent you think they are; if they are not the right fit, then they are not the right fit. Don't try to force someone into an organization just because they seem to be a good technologist. That is a recipe for a very bored programmer and an unhappy team.

Similarly, don't dismiss a candidate out of hand just because you don't perfectly prefer their resume; have a conversation with everyone. At worst, you will waste 15 minutes of your day, and at best you might find a diamond in the rough. Also, (and this is the part that requires just a little bit of intuition) don't be too strict on your positional requirements. You don't need the perfect candidate (titans of technology are quite rare finds), you need the right candidate that fits with the team at the right time. For example, don't be afraid to hire a junior Ruby developer for a mid-level PHP position if you truly believe that they can do the job; hell, I wouldn't be afraid to hire a junior Ruby developer for a senior leadership position if I truly believed they had the personal and professional chops to do it. Every person is different, every skillset is unique, and a good manager has to apply a little judgment.

If you work hard and pay close attention, hiring a quality team will become the greatest thing you ever do. It will lower your stress levels, it will raise productivity, and it will keep everyone happy. It is truly the most important thing you will do as you grow your start-up for the future.

QUICK TIPS

1. Six phases of team growth
2. Management changes at each level
3. Prepare for uncomfortable shifts
4. Ride the waves and roll with the punches

THE TEAMS

In addition to the importance of hiring engineers, I think it's important to spend a little time talking about overall team organization and growth.

In my experience, there are five distinct phases of technical team development that a start-up will experience (assuming they are successful). The first phase is the simplest and easiest to manage (and the most likely to be overseen by only a founder):

All Hands On Deck!

Typically, this phase will only last a brief while, and it is here that a team will have little or no formal organization (and often no formal process). The team is very small (maybe two or three people at the most) and everyone is working aggressively in the same direction, functioning as a single unit, like a living organism. There's no team or tech lead, no dedicated product team, no QA team, no concept of junior or senior engineer; there is just a bunch of guys (and gals) that have a singular mission and not enough hours in the day in which to accomplish their goals. Individual tasks are often assigned by simply shouting at each other from across the room; late nights and weekends are too common, coffee is abundant, and very little strategic planning is ever undertaken. Both critical to business success and dangerous to future prosperity, the most successful companies will spend only enough time at this phase to afford the second phase.

TECH Team 6!

It is at this phase that the first germinations of real organization and process will begin to take shape. With each new hire, an informal hierarchy will begin to emerge within the original core of engineers, as those with natural leadership skills begin to use them to lead. The group will still be mostly flat and cohesive, but there will be a sense of lateral respect toward seniors. There will still be no formal quality assurance process (beyond simple test-driven development and basic automation), but systems will come into focus. Code will now be versioned in git or svn, and future deployments will become less chaotic as customers arrive. The group will still function largely without a strict process, but individuals will begin to gravitate toward areas of development that they most enjoy (frontend, systems, design, UI/UX, support). A good founder will encourage this evolution and specialization, allowing the burgeoning leaders to assign work to the newcomers and approve code for deployment. As they assume some ownership over the product, the founder can take note of whether or not they are suited for a higher role in the future.

Twelve Angry Engineers

As the team grow further still, the hierarchy will deepen and formalize, and the need for real process and management will start to come into focus. Between 8 and 12 team members, the group can no longer function on informal methods alone; the code will start to fray and become a little difficult to deploy, bugs will make it into production, and output will slightly drop.

Leaders must start to think strategically. It is here that an intelligent founder will either discover their inner manager and embody the leader, or they will hire a professional and influence from afar. Whichever is assumed, those who are responsible will institute the first genuine rules. The team will be broken into two or more groups (likely frontend and backend, or database and service, etc.) and team leads will be publicly assigned to govern groupings of two to four. The distinction between junior and senior will strengthen, and some mentorship will be casually encouraged by task and project assignment.

The first stages of the Agile conversion will take

place here. The first planning sessions will occur, a daily stand-up will be instituted, and a multi-week sprint will be introduced (although often ignored in the face of deadlines and outside pressures).

Hail Corporate!

Serious financing will now be in place (at least a Series A), and the company has some meaningful revenue. The hiring strategy is now aggressive and constant. As the team expands up to and beyond twenty, several distinct teams will come into focus by area of responsibility, and the original set of engineers will have found their permanent roles.

A true leader will be critical at this phase; an improperly managed team dynamic can choke productivity and create insurmountable challenges in process and procedure. Agile methods will now be rigidly in place. A product team (either dedicated or composed of members of business) will start worrying itself with a grander vision and strategic roadmap. The technical leadership will have to work more closely with product to develop a set of engineering goals and milestones, which will be broken into epics and user stories. The first review process will take place to build internal teams that best suit the interests and goals of members.

Quality assurance will become a real thing now. Deployment procedures will be taken away from engineers and given to the testing team. Technical leads will now spend more time managing than in the code (although they will still do a little of both), and the departmental leader will be a pure manager.

There may be some unhappiness amongst the original team, likely over a lack of promotion or a loss of the start-up culture (or other reasons), and some may choose to leave. The leadership will need to be ruthless in enforcing release dates to avoid feature-creep and deadline slip as release plans become more critical to customers and sales efforts. Eventually a rhythm will start to develop, and each individual unit will start acting autonomously and seemlessly: backend engineers will be able to focus on systems and data improvements, the frontend team will be able to focus on feature requests and business support, design and UI/UX will be able to focus on consumer-facing development, and the QA team will do what it does best to find and solve problems. All the parts will know their role in the whole and function according to direction.

The Oiled Giant

In great success, a team can expand to the point that the highest levels of management only ever interact with subordinate managers. The developers are kept away from the departmental leadership; trust becomes critically important. The technical leaders need to now be rockstars who really know their engineers and are able to predict their output reliably and maintain productivity. Turnover will become a little more common, and maintaining a pipeline of talent while adhering to good hiring practices is crucial. The development process will now be mostly academic, with little to no noticeable deviation from the expectation. There is an ironclad distinction between junior, senior, and lead, with selective promotions for those who demonstrate excellence beyond their station. Product is very formal now, and will often consist of many ex-technologists that understand the limitation of a system without having to be in the weeds or a bother to the engineers. For the biggest groups, technology might even be completely segregated from business. The separation between layers of managers and leads can create problems, and regular all-department events can ensure a feeling of belonging amongst the members.

Many companies successfully ride the waves through the five phases, and a few even do so with the same leadership in place at all levels. But it is far more common for leaders to cycle in and out, with each person having a specialty. And you must be okay with this (especially for founders). Some leaders prefer to work in tight-knit teams, while some prefer to work with a select bunch of trusted leads; some prefer to work with very large and distributed teams, and some prefer an intimate setting. It will be the responsibility of the board to recognize flaws in the existing management (if there happens to be any) and introduce stronger leadership that is equipped to handle the growth. The transition between each phase is the most dangerous period (the dreaded **J-curve** of lost productivity), but can be successfully navigated to form a rock-solid company.

QUICK TIPS

1. Process is not corporate (bad)
2. Agile is your friend!
3. Let developers develop
4. Plan, then adapt as needed

PROCESS

The start-up is a technology religion, and process is the devil. Young companies often pride themselves on their free-wheelin' attitudes: no set hours, no meetings, no code reviews, no quality assurance, everyone works individually in harmony and unison toward a common cause! This faithful adherence to nothing is often reinforced through early success, as a process-free environment can yield impressive results when the team is very small and composed mostly of founding members. If you put three or four competent and ambitious people in a small room, you will be amazed at how quickly they can achieve; however, when that team grows to ten, twenty, or thirty people, and they are working on a code base twice the size and spread between triple the clients, you are going to suddenly discover the love and beauty of a good process.

Don't worry; **it's really not the devil!**

Process is not the drab corporate offices, ties, and curmudgeonly middle-managers you imagine it to be; process is merely the method by which the visionaries of the company are able to direct the team and keep track of progress. A good executive can weave process into a start-up almost unnoticed, just a handful of new tasks during the week and a few quick meet-ups to check in. Personally, I am a fan of a version of the Agile process, which puts much of the onus of review on the management and/or product team, and leaves the developers to develop. How it works:

1. Meet annually, quarterly, or monthly with the big players and talk about overarching strategy. Take notes on a white board and break down exactly what you hope to accomplish in the next year, quarter, or month. Once you have your wish-list, try to disassemble those grand ideas into large but distinct chunks of work (called epic stories), and store your detail in your task management program (there are many; I recommend Rally or Jira). Once you have these in place, create sub-stories that identify single iterations of work within the epic; for instance, if the epic is "building a car," stories might be "build the carburetor," "inflate the tires," "install the air bag," etc. Sort these stories by importance and in needed order, and assign rough workload estimates (called points). Once you feel you have a reasonable breakdown of work for the next chunk of

time, you can start your weekly planning session.

2. At the beginning of each week, spend half an hour in the early morning with team leads (or, for small squads, the entire team) and pull stories out of the backlog and into the sprint by ordering until you have a full set of work. Give developers a half hour to task the stories (or do it as a group if you wish) and then reconvene to review the upcoming sprint. If anyone is truly overloaded, push some stories into the next sprint, or pull them back into the backlog. Once complete, each developer should have their set of weekly assignments and can be set loose.

3. For the rest of the week, meet very quickly in the developer area for ten to fifteen minutes and discuss how the sprint is going. Keep this meeting to three questions: what did you work on yesterday, what are you working on today, and do you have any blockers that require assistance? If the sprint is running smoothly, and the teams are kept to a reasonable size, the stand-up might take five minutes or less. The purpose of this daily check-in is to give the developers a consistent opportunity to voice concerns and struggles, solicit for further information or help, or ask for more work.

4. At the end of the day on Friday, institute a code freeze, notate any incomplete work, send completed work along to the QA squad (if you have one), and hold a very brief postmortem. The purpose of the postmortem is only to voice any concerns over the prior sprint: were there any problems that need addressing, or was anyone over-

or under-scheduled? Just get a quick sense of how the team is feeling so that you can better approach the Monday-morning planning session, and address any concerns before the next bucket of work begins.

If done correctly, this process should occupy very little of a developer's time. During a successful sprint, the total weekly time commitment might be just an hour or two. Outside of the few gatherings and discussions, the development crew can be as free-wheelin' and unstructured as they choose. So long as the alloted work is completed on time and in good condition, it shouldn't matter how that work is accomplished. Let your crew work in whatever way allows them to be most productive; everyone has their own style, and you want to nurture what makes each person successful.

When the team gets sufficiently large and starts to include developers of varying skill, you may choose to implement more structured code reviews and one-on-one sessions, but that can probably be avoided in the early days (or done discreetly and informally by the leadership).

Don't fear process!

Do it right, and the team will soar!

QUICK TIPS

1. Be gentle, honest, and humble
2. Always try to correct first
3. Inform and educate along the way
4. Reassure the team and be respectful

FIRING

There is a single topic in the whole of the business world, and especially in the start-up work, from managers to executives, to founders and Presidents, that seemingly no one wants to talk about; and yet all eventually partake. It is the proverbial elephant in the room, the emperor without clothes, the fictional redrafting of reality that keeps the office world running smooth and steady.

The tragedy of this quite deliberate ignorance, however, is that it has generated many generations of leadership failure and employee malcontent, as well as has ruined the early days of many start-up founders; and these are failures that could be solved through some simple conversation and compassion. The topic I am referencing, and would like to carefully discuss, is of course the occasional (and unfortunate) need to fire someone.

As I have said before, and still strongly believe, the most important thing a manager will do, at any level of leadership, is to hire. This is especially important in a start-up, when every hire is critical. The most effective way to avoid the discomfort of a future firing is to work diligently and carefully toward ensuring that each new hire is a good hire, that each new team member is coming into the company with purpose, capability, and passion.

However, if you happen to find yourself in any position of leadership for long enough, you will eventually find yourself having to fire someone. I don't want to bum you out, but that is just the way the world tends to work. Perhaps the company is experiencing a difficult stretch of revenue and needs to make some cutbacks (the dreaded "layoff"), or perhaps an employee, despite efforts to correct, has consistently underperformed and must be replaced. Whatever the reason may be, firing is never easy, it is always painful, and you should always feel that there was no other option.

Before we talk about the act of firing itself, let's talk just a little bit about dealing with behavioral correction. Unlike a layoff or a disciplinary action, which is often the result of circumstances beyond your immediate control, a performance-based firing can often be avoided through an internal program of correction. This is especially true in the technology world, where logic and critical thinking are the tools of the trade (and occasionally are in need of some sharpening). A good manager will be in regular contact with his subordinates, and will be willing to talk candidly and directly about any issues that might arise. If you find that one of your employees is struggling, it is important that you convey your displeasure immediately and privately. This is not a matter of anger or disappointment, but just an honest assessment of the situation. Explain what the problem is, and ask for feedback; is there something wrong? Perhaps a life event has sidelined their focus, or maybe they are working with a new technology or standard in which they are unfamiliar. Whatever the problem, be sure to isolate the root cause and develop a plan for correction.

If an employee is facing a skills gap, schedule time to meet one-on-one and do a little mentoring; or send the employee to a class or conference on the subject. If this is fiscally impractical, as may be the case for particularly small and unfinanced start-ups, seek out inexpensive options, such as books and free lectures. Give the employee the tools and opportunity to showcase their ability to learn, and their desire to improve. Sometimes the difference between success and failure can just be a little bit of education and experience.

On the other hand, if the employee is facing an unrelated issue (perhaps some trouble at home, or a medical problem, or a legal matter), discuss their options and try to find a mutually acceptable solution. Perhaps the employee just needs some time off from work to deal with their troubles; this may especially be true if the issue is medical, as a leave of absence might help the employee focus on getting healthy. Whatever the issue may be, be sure to address it directly and compassionately, and put serious effort into finding a path forward. A full-time employee should be a long-term commitment, and a few weeks of instability can be weathered if it will result in years of rock-star performance. There may unfortunately be less wiggle room for some particularly small and early start-ups that have very slim margins for error, but even then some effort should be taken to find success.

As you work towards a correction, meet with the troubled employee as often as you're able. Give them regular feedback about their progress, and continually mentor them in areas that still need improvement. If, after some time and discussion, it becomes clear that the problem cannot be solved, it should not be a surprise to anyone that the moment of firing has arrived; everyone should be well aware of the state of things at every step of the process.

If that unfortunate day does arrive, remember to maintain your compassion. Unless the firing is due to an unforgivable misbehavior, there is likely no "bad guy" in this scenario; the employee is simply not fit or capable of handling their duties properly, and you have specific needs that must be fulfilled. Rather than the overt aggression that is commonly implied in the word "firing," I like to think of these matters as (and please forgive the Political Correct-ness) "employee relocations."

In service of this idealistic vision, I almost

always offer the individual at least two weeks notice prior to the forced departure (during which I expect the employee to hunt for their next job), and provide them with an honest disclosure and explanation on the matter. Always have this conversation privately and at the end of the day; allow the employee to go home afterwards, as even the most measured and expected departure will likely leave the employee wanting to be away from the office. Inform the rest of team in a private in-person meeting, and explain that the outgoing employee will continue to work for a few weeks more and will transition their responsibilities to other team members.

Never, ever, *ever* disparage a fired employee, especially in front of the team!

After you inform the team as a group, have a private conversation with each of your team leaders (or, for particularly small start-ups, with each team member) and discuss the situation candidly. Make sure they know that their own jobs are not threatened, that the company is still strong and moving forward, and answer any questions that do not denigrate the former employee.

Firing someone is horrible.

No matter how deserved or unavoidable, and no matter how many times you go through the process, you will feel terrible afterwards; don't worry, this is normal. But if you truly made an honest effort to help and support a struggling employee, or were faced with a circumstance that you genuinely were not able to control, and so long as you treated the departure with tact and humility, then you should be able to eventually take comfort in knowing that you did what you had to, and everything you could.

> **QUICK TIPS**
>
> 1. Ignore the popular ideals
> 2. Hire smart, capable people
> 3. Create a fun, collaborative environment
> 4. Relax; it will all work out in the end.

CULTURE

"Start-up Culture" is a phrase that seems to hold a surprisingly public and universal understanding.

Even for those who have yet to work within one, or will never work within one, almost anyone can outline the stereotypical characteristics of a start-up whenever they are asked:

1. A fun, youthful, quirky, and motivated group of people who don't shower enough.

2. An open, modern work space and a comfortable, informal atmosphere.

3. No dress code, a non-existent processes, and a wild-eyed and crazy (but genius) founder.

4. Really long working hours, and a high-stress, high-turnover environment.

5. Relatively low pay, yet exceptional equity, paid time off, and health benefits.

6. Free coffee, snacks, and (of course) alcohol.

7. Foosball.

That is but a few of the assumptions that I have heard in recent years; and many are admittedly not wrong (even if somewhat embellished). This public knowledge is partly due to the growing popularity of the great start-up story within the entertainment industry ("The Social Network," "Silicon Valley," "Jobs," etc.), and partially due to the relentless media coverage of the annual parade of tech IPO or acquisition events (Facebook, twitter, WhatsApp, etc). Unfortunately, the ubiquity of understanding has created a common solicitation amongst first-time (and sometimes serial) entrepreneurs:

"How do I create good start-up culture?"

Let me start by expressing my belief that there is *no such thing* as a true ideal for company culture. Stereotypes aside, nearly every company (even those of whom I would vigorously argue embody the traditional spirit of the start-up) has it's own unique signature. There is not a hard line between high-corporate and the scrappy small; you can exist anywhere in between and should feel comfortable with your occupation.

Furthermore, a really good culture is not truly something you can forcibly create so much as it is something you foster socially (although you can assist it's arrival, as I will discuss later). It's a little like building a band; to make good music you need to bring together individuals that fit with the style and can immediately play well together.

Put another way: Your company will only be able to achieve the culture of the people that work for it (including yourself). You ultimately have only yourself and your hiring methods as a path to your goal culture, and you should take equal care in both.

This is one of the many reasons why I put so much emphasis on hiring as the central concern of any good technical manager or founder (as I've now mentioned too many times). *The team is everything!* I will always advocate for a very broad approach to talent screening, and the hiring of the "right fit" engineers, as opposed to just criterion-based formal vetting. A brilliant, high-credentialed engineer with a poor personality and poor work ethic will never match the value of a young intelligent engineer with boundless enthusiasm and a desire to succeed!

Now, while I do contend that you cannot force culture change by executive edict, you can, in the service of the mission of good talent acquisition, do a number of things to help attract the best. For instance, you can establish an exciting overall work environment (a foosball table, while not crucial, certainly can't hurt). You want candidates to feel welcomed from the moment they step into the space and introduce themselves.

I would also recommend choosing an open work

environment (avoid high-walled cubicles or corner offices), as the best engineers I've worked with all love to be a part of a real collaboration, to feel an identity with a common team.

Take care in your own management style.

While an open office space might be able to sell an ideal of collaboration at first sight, an astute candidate will quickly recognize a gimmick when they see one. You don't want to just look like you're collaborative, you want to *be* collaborative! A

lways involve your employees in key decisions (no one likes the feeling of being out of the loop), take your team to lunch or other group events from time to time, and always be willing to lend a helping hand (or ear) when you are needed. Be a mentor to your team where possible. The best leaders are often also the best listeners. And those who work with great leaders will sell that vision to others, both consciously and unconsciously, and it will show in each candidate they meet.

Finally, the best advice I can offer is: **Relax!**

The origins of the "Start-up Culture" are found in young founders with limited experience with working with smart people to do the impossible with no time to spare. That collaborative root and open environment that are now so famous are rarely deliberate decisions, but rather products of necessity and urgency. If you are in a position to consider how best to create a comparable culture without the panic of the pre-revenue, pre-product displeasure of a very early start-up, then you are doing alright. Be yourself, be a part of your own team, and hold onto your passion, and the culture will find itself.

QUICK TIPS

1. Don't panic!
2. Find your strengths and weaknesses
3. Consult with team and advisors
4. Find a path forward through talent

PIVOT

One of the most painful moments in the life of a founder will be when they realize that their brilliant idea, the original reason for the very existence of their current start-up, the vision that they had fought and sweat and bled and cried so valiantly in defense of, is actually untenable and in need of revision.

Entrepreneurs are passionate people; they may exude a veneer of professionalism, but underneath that business exterior lies the soul of a hobbyist and a fanatic. To pour such love and affection into a venture only to find out that your great hypothesis is hopelessly flawed can be psychologically crippling. The saloons of America are today filled with so many anxious founders trying to drink their way to a resolution and reassurance.

But I say, fear not!

The best companies are champions of change; the best founders learn to swim with the current; the greatest successes are often birthed out of failure. When you find yourself pitted against a failing concept, put on the brakes and try to pivot.

But to where do we pivot?

This is not an easy question to answer. In order to find the necessary path forward you will need to evaluate your exact position. Not every pivot is a complete reversal of direction; you may find that you simply need a slight course correction.

Perhaps your revenue model is insufficient and you need to find a new capitalization strategy; perhaps your product is too bloated and simply needs some tightening and design focus; or perhaps you just need to shift primary efforts from one customer to another. Develop an analysis of the fundamental problem you were originally trying to solve and how your existing product is working to solve it; where are the gaps? Is there a flaw in your original analysis? Perhaps the problem you set out to solve isn't worth solving, after all; is there a related problem that could be worth tackling?

Examine the entire space, put a stern, critical eye towards the strengths and weaknesses of your current team and system, and start creating lists. A great example of the power of the pivot comes from Facebook, which was initially a school-based closed ecosystem. Before they opened their software to the wide world, there surely was a lot of tough internal analysis and decision-making over the value of a school-only workflow. In the end, a pivot to an open platform made the company the financial and social juggernaut that it is today.

If after your analysis you find that you are in need of a complete pivot, I still will argue that all is not yet lost. As hard as this may be to believe, the company is not really the product; the company is you and the staff. The reason why investors focus so much on the team, as opposed to just the idea, is because the team is where the ultimate value lies. Investors know that a large numbers of companies will need to pivot and change business models at some point in time, and those companies with intelligent, ambitious, flexible, and passionate team members willing to do whatever is necessary for success will best be able to weather the changes.

Put your best people in a room with a white board and start brainstorming; think about what you've built, the industry, the market forces, and what problems you think need solving. Consider your customers (if you have any), your investors, your media influence. Where are you best able to solve a problem that needs solving.

But how do you know when you need to pivot?

This is the hardest question of all. It is often frustrating how much of the start-up experience is not quantitative (especially for mathematical brains, like myself), but the ugly truth of the matter is that the answer lies in the gut and an intuitive analysis of progress. There is something to be said for the occasional steadfast commitment to a vision even in the face of adversity. Very few start-ups will stand and sail to victory right out of the gate. It is the task of the entrepreneur to get a handle on the progress of the business and critically analyze what it has accomplished and must accomplish. Get feedback from your board of advisors, your investors, your team, your friends, and your family. Take their criticism with a pinch of humility, and take notes.

If at any point you find yourself ready to pivot, especially in a way that substantially alters the business model and the product, be sure to include your entire team at every step of the process. It will take a lot of effort from everyone, at all levels of expertise, to accomplish a quick shift in vision, and there will likely be a lot of discomfort.

Never forget that a pivot involves discarding a great deal of work that your team may have sunk a great deal of pride into; nurture their feelings and don't be afraid to express understanding. Rally the troops and make sure that they know that the company is still committed to success, committed to the team, and will do what it takes to ride adversity through to victory. A start-up is like a club, and everyone needs to feel like they belong.

Don't be afraid of change;

it can be critical to success!

QUICK TIPS

1. Personnel shifts are tough
2. Leverage recruiters and your network
3. Be judicious but swift
4. Keep the team informed!

SCALING

If you have ever enjoyed a time with a successful technology start-up, then you will undoubtedly have many interesting tales of growth and pain, from working in a basement closet with only a few close friends, all the way to landing that fifth major client and moving into that fourth office space.

Having myself worked in three such adventures, I can attest that the path to greatness is strange, difficult, and curiously predictable. The nuance of the travel is always unique to each venture, but the primary issue is always the same: how to scale! And this is nearly always a human-specific problem.

I don't want to just gloss over the inevitable struggles of an expanding technology platform, as they will exist and will be many, but typically the worst pain points in the growth of a start-up are not technological. A good core of quality engineers should be able to build an infrastructure that can handle the first several rounds of customer infusion, and issues can be triaged in manageable chunks of effort. The exception, of course, is the lucky service that experiences sudden and crushing growth due to social popularity, but that is not the norm. Rather, the critical pain point is almost always personnel.

1. How fast should you hire new talent?

2. Who do you hire, and how to find them?

3. How do you maintain company culture?

4. How do you keep employees happy?

5. How do you retain your team through shifts in process and structure?

Even in a struggling economy, the top talent is difficult to find and difficult to keep. In a thriving economy, that talent can become almost non-existent, and when available can be prohibitively expensive. An established company with moderate growth can often weather these searches with patience and virtue; but in a high-growth start-up, it is not unusual to encounter an immediate and critical need for several high-profile positions, and patience can run very thin.

The temptation to hire anyone that submits a decent looking resume can become overwhelming. It is at this stage that every talent search must target only the best caliber individuals with the broadest array of skills. You want to cast a very wide net; I highly recommend leveraging your network as thoroughly as possible. Develop a rapport with the best recruiters, and stick close to those you can trust to bring quality candidates with reasonable salary demands. When possible, be prepared to pay top dollar for the right person. It may stretch the times between hires and may threaten your budget, but each hire of top-tier talent will be more impactful, more productive, and more excellent in a wider area of needs, and the right person can transform a team. Reserve the junior hires for after a solid core of culturally-cohesive seniors are reaching their limits.

The other personnel concern that arrives through rapid growth is the dreaded culture shift. It is very common for the earliest team members to be those who love and thrive in an unbounded start-up culture. They relish the back-room development, the stress and anguish of unrealistic deadlines, and the promise of immediate and thrilling result.

For a company to succeed, this frantic pace must find a balance, and as the company matures and expands these individuals will be the most difficult individuals to keep happy and satisfied. Because they are so talented and cool under pressure, it is right to want to keep them pleased and working cheerily. In service of this goal, it is best to be cautious with the hiring of managers; try to focus on hands-on leaders that can maintain the trust and loyalty of the core talent. Encourage an environment of collaboration, even when team size makes true collaboration a real struggle; and always keep the team well-informed of company progress. Start-up talent wants to be engaged, to be connected with the business, and to feel the impact of their efforts; it's why they like it small!

Every venture will encounter highs and lows as they grow, and every rapid expansion will feel more painful than joyful. But there is a comfort in pain due to growth; it gives promise of a bright future and makes the effort worth every struggle. While the start-up world is not for everyone, for anyone that can handle the race I actively encourage them to play. You'll rarely regret it!

QUICK TIPS

1. It's not good to have no strategy
2. Don't rely on "viral" content
3. Be social, be genuine, be engaging
4. Be consistent in everything

MARKETING

Promotional efforts will always represent the very last thoughts of a start-up team, or worse. There has developed this unconscious sentiment of sexiness around the missing marketing strategy, and it can be very damaging to success.

When expressed, the argument against having a marketing strategy is usually centered around the idea that any well-built product will succeed on it's social virality alone. In other words, if the masses won't share it, then the failure is in the product and not the promotional effort.

Unfortunately, this line of thinking can cripple high-quality ventures that might have otherwise succeeded. The dark, terrible reality is that social momentum is a complex beast that is difficult to predict (and even more difficult to engineer) and impossible to initiate without assistance. The web is vast wasteland with limited natural discoverability, and if you don't put yourself in front of as many eyes as possible as deliberately as possible, then you won't find all that much organic growth.

Perhaps this requires emphasis:

Have a marketing strategy!

Keep in mind that the word "strategy" probably comes across a little more grandiose than it should; I am not recommending that you spend your entire seed or Angel round on advertisements and Super Bowl commercials. Most young businesses do not require the services of an agency, or even a CMO. In fact, a good marketing effort for a young start-up can easily involve very little (or even zero) money at all. There are numerous ways to get your product in front of potential customers that are easy and inexpensive, and only require a sustained effort and a consistent presentation.

But you have to make the effort!

A good and relatively easy method for garnering some early exposure is to create a "press release." Similar to the word "strategy" said in the previous paragraph, this sounds a little more complicated than it actually is. All you will be doing is penning a few paragraphs that quickly explain something you recently did, and then sending that document around to relevant publications.

For example, if you happen to be a brand new venture, you could put together a press release that simply explains what you do and announces your existence. If you release a new feature or product, you can talk a little about what it is and why it was made. And the best press releases will center around customers (a key acquisition, a glowing review, or a major new partner) and will tell a very short and interesting story. Once you have something put together, you can either use a distribution service (and there are many free or cheap options, such as PRWeb) or you can selectively target publications.

I highly recommend the targeted approach; you should find publications that have interests that are closely aligned with your product and tailor your release for a specific editor or reporter. This will maximize your chances of getting noticed, and will create the most value for your effort. It may also help develop an early relationship with important individuals that will help you in the long term.

Another important undertaking involves putting regular effort into community engagement. There exists a dangerous habit of reclusion in much of the start-up world, and it can be very isolating. While you may suffer the urge to work in your garage, head down coding at all times, 24/7, you must pull yourself out of the darkness once in a while and get outside where the people are.

Go to conferences, meet-ups, and other relevant gatherings and talk some about what you do. If the opportunity arises, host a lecture or presentation; pass around your business card and chit-chat with the people of your industry. Similar to generic job searching, networking is crucial to success.

It is also necessary to put energy into a social media strategy. While there may be romance in the idea of having the internet discover and spread your product independently, the reality is that the most successful viral campaigns are orchestrated at the beginning by an effort to expose.

Create accounts on all the major social networks and post content regularly. Engage the communities of these services and be genuine, interesting, and helpful (spam is almost never tolerated anywhere, and is never effective). For example, if you are creating a new music sharing service, I recommend you become active in music forums on reddit. Don't just talk about your specific product or service, and instead become known as an expert. Comment on popular postings and offer some insight. You want your name and brand to become associated with the core category of your business. As your following grows, your shared materials will reach further into the ether of the internet. There is no way to know where the threshold lies, but eventually something you share will find a life of it's own and start to spread (the glorious "viral" item). Don't try to force it; it has to happen naturally.

Finally, but most importantly, make sure every form of product presentation is consistent, easy to understand, and easy to consume. You need a logo and a business name that is very memorable and interesting. Your website, mobile app, letter head, coffee mugs, pens, mouse pads, and t-shirts should all share the same color scheme and font style. Your website should have enough explanatory text to understand what your product is and how to use it, but not so much to be onerous to read and enjoy. And your product should be simple, effective, and worth using to everyone in your target audience. A lot of this must be completed before the first piece of marketing is given to the first potential consumer (and good user experience should be woven into the architecture of the product from day one), but keep revisiting your materials so you can make sure that everything remains consistent as you grow.

Marketing should not be a scary or boring word to an entrepreneur. Some of the best entrepreneurs of the modern era have been excellent salesmen (and saleswomen) at their core, and they have put marketing on a pedestal without failing at product. Marketing efforts, when done correctly, will not detract from the company vision or the quality of the service. Rather, it will enhance them and bring customers, the lifeblood of a new venture. Don't suffer a loss to an inferior company with better outreach! Be the best on every front!

QUICK TIPS

1. Growth can be both great and painful
2. Prepare yourself for the new role
3. Use the team and board to find talent
4. Embrace change!

THE NEW CEO

If you should someday find yourself in possession of a start-up that is experiencing any serious success (and revenue), then it is very likely that you will also someday find yourself reconsidering your role within your own company.

While there certainly exists a handful of notable ventures that have managed to retain a single CEO from start-up to exit (Groupon was a notable and popular example prior to the ousting of Andrew Mason), they should be regarded as the exceptions rather than the rule. The odds are quite high that you will eventually have to strip yourself of the coveted title and find somewhere else to direct your talents. Unless you happen to be a business titan and are confident in the steadfast maintenance of your top-level leadership, I highly recommend you start mentally preparing yourself for this process, as it can be surprisingly devastating to a founder.

It is important to recognize that this coming role change is not at all a negative reflection on your creative and critical abilities. In fact, it should be considered a hallmark of your success; without much outside assistance (and likely without much money), you have managed to take a simple idea and a tiny team and catapult it all into the realm of serious business. That is quite an achievement that many others have failed to match!

By the time you are considering an outside CEO, you almost certainly will have at least a few non-founding employees, some customers, a nice office environment, profit, maybe some investment, and a fully functioning company; unfortunately, it is very difficult to take such a burgeoning success and push it over that first productivity j-curve and realize the hockey-sticks of growth. It is much safer and cheaper to task that to someone else, someone who is in possession of the relevant experience to navigate that hump, rather than try to do it yourself.

The growth of any company tends to experience waves of productivity and management stress. For example, at the very beginning of any new venture, productivity will be very high and the company will run smooth and fast; the team is small, focused, and unified, and there are not yet any bottlenecks for growth. As the first round of success arrives, output might increase even faster with the first few non-founding senior-level hires. Founders will here start to feel invincible as they watch the needle move steadily and constantly, believing further expansion to be inevitable and eternal.

But as you continue to hire and expand the team in order to meet an ever-increasing customer base and demand, productivity will unfortunately start to plateau; it happens to almost every company. You'll find it increasingly difficult to manage the size of the team and maintain a consistent and coherent strategy, especially as the group starts to split and form teams with diverging purpose. Eventually you'll find that further hiring actually brings about a surprising decrease in overall productivity, as they are only able to exist as bottlenecks, consuming management time and energy and creating team confusion; the company has grown too large and is in need of experienced management to refocus.

This is the first j-curve (there are more to come), and it is at this point that a founder should seek outside help. There are a number of excellent early-stage CEOs that solely specialize in helping young, venture-backed, successful companies rearrange their team dynamic, install the first top-down process, and recruit further talent from the field. In finding such a person, it is highly recommended that you immediately involve your investors and advisors; they very likely have a network filled with such professionals, and could save you a lot of time and headache. Be sure to have the whole team meet with each candidate. You will generate a lot of goodwill and respect, and avoid some turnover, if the employees are given a vote and a voice in the selection of their new boss.

And stay away from any big name candidates, regardless of their genuine interest level; top talent is very expensive, comes with a lot of unforeseeable baggage, and there are exceptional individuals on the rise and available for far less.

As the company is finding and preparing for the new CEO, the founder will need to take some time to evaluate their purpose. Relinquishing that CEO label should not diminish their status, and may even help strengthen their abilities. A founder with a technical background may find that shedding the need to manage operational issues helps them focus on building a world-class product; such a founder may find themselves better suited for the CTO position. A founder with a sales background may find that no longer involving themselves in product management helps them build a stellar crew and improve customer retention; such a founder may find themselves better suited as a VP of Sales. Give yourself some time, make some lists, and honestly evaluate yourself, then make your recommendation.

It will also be important for the founding team to keep close to the new CEO in the early months of the transition. This new executive will bring some experience and abilities that you don't have, but you will also have insider knowledge on the company, team, product, and market that the new CEO couldn't possibly yet have. For quite a while, you will be operating as a unit, co-CEOs in practice (even if not in name), building a focused vision through open collaboration and discussion. No top-level transition is ever immediate, and a smooth transition will never end up with a clean and total break. You are still the founder, and you are still critical to the eventual success of the venture.

Changing roles can be painful and upsetting, but if done correctly it can make the company stronger, grow faster, and help you achieve your ultimate vision in a way not otherwise possible.

Embrace change; it can be invigorating!

> **QUICK TIPS**
>
> 1. This is the goal of all start-ups
> 2. Don't rush it; it will come when it comes
> 3. Decide what you want to do afterwards
> 4. Focus on operations as the exit unfolds

EXIT

Imagine:

You have spent years toiling in a closet-sized office, taking home a meager salary (or no salary at all) in return for a ninety-hour work week and non-stop stress; you've knocked on every door, window, and wall looking for new clients and customers, and you've utterly exhausted your network in search of financing, mentorship, and growth potential.

Now, you've finally realized some success, your company is making some real money, and you have investors. Eventually, the blessed day should arrive when an opportunity to realize an exit event will present itself. Whether this is a choice to go public, merge with another company, or get acquired, the end-goal of every start-up is to eventually reach this point of prosperity. It is what all the blood, sweat, and tears has been leading toward.

The great reward at the end of the struggle!

Never forget that an exit doesn't mean the end of the line. While there are some "unhappy" exits (such as a fire-sale liquidation at failure), a good company will keep running long after the investors and founders have gotten their return on investment.

But an exit is still a critical and special moment in the history of a company, and can often have a profound impact on how the business evolves. For instance, public companies will suddenly find that they are at the mercy of an expanded scrutiny by a wider body of investors and regulators; they will be very concerned with how revenue is managed and the company is directed, and will eventually expect dividends. Similarly, acquired companies may need to re-brand or change core functionality to match the new ownership. Merged companies, meanwhile, may find internal cultural conflicts as the two entities learn to co-exist and operate efficiently. Prior to the exit, you will find decisions to be simpler and less bureaucratic. In fact, complications from the exit are common reasons for the departure of founding members, off into the sunset to build another venture and enjoy the fruits and perils of the start-up world yet again.

You will have to decide what is best for you.

It is also worth mentioning that you will have to safeguard the rewards of an exit many years before the fateful day arrives (as we discussed previously). Take care with how you construct your cap table, guard your equity jealously (but not excessively so), and keep careful track of all your progress. Keep meeting minutes, bootstrap for as long as you are able, and be careful with how often and how substantially you dilute your holdings. Keep copies of every contract and agreement you sign, and notate all your expenses, personal investments, and other financial issues. You will need to be in excellent shape for both the initial investments (from angel investors, seed funds, and venture capital firms) as well as in preparation for any exit; accountants won't accept anything less than full documentation when dealing with such money, and you don't want any last minute surprises.

Don't get overly excited when the first sightings of an exit start to surface. All liquidity events require an arduous effort and take a great amount of time to negotiate, process, and complete. From the first moment you hear of an opportunity, expect a full year or more to pass before the actual event is within sight, if it arrives at all.

With public offerings, be prepared to spend time schmoozing investors and handling your road show. Depending on your particular strengths, your eyes might be best kept on operations, doing what you do best, and letting the lawyers and investment bankers manage the transaction. But even with your focus on day-to-day needs, always keep aware of the summary and make sure the best interests of the company are being respected.

The exit is a crucial milestone in the progression of any start-up, and when it arrives it is sure to make an entrepreneur sing for joy. Before it arrives, however, be sure to keep your eye on the ball and let the end-goal arrive on it's own schedule.

> **QUICK TIPS**
>
> 1. Decide what you want to do
> 2. Don't be afraid to do it all again
> 3. Focus on the fun and joy
> 4. Have another adventure!

THE NEXT THING

One of the most difficult moments in the life of an entrepreneur will come at the end of the mission: the company has been built, molded, grown, and expanded; you have staff and revenue and brand recognition; an exit has come and gone, and the company is now public or has been purchased, and it now represents an oiled corporate machine.

It is no longer your baby, your pet, your start-up. It is now bigger than you, beyond you, humming like a jet engine and flying with you. It may now be time to move on to the next thing!

Okay, maybe I'm getting ahead of myself.

Not everyone is to be a serial entrepreneur. You may decide to stick with your original creation until the bitter end, happy in your now ever-expanding corporate beast. But this is not the typical life cycle of a founder. The enthusiasm, energy, and passion that is an entrepreneurial prerequisite does not do well outside the chaos of a start-up. It is typical for a founder to find themselves itching for the glory days of late-night panic sessions, coffee-fueled pitch bonanzas, and an endless stream of code. And if you have that itch, I urge you to scratch.

Do it all again!

Just like the first time, there is no guarantee of further success. One successful start-up does not ensure another, or any others. However, there are a few benefits to building a second start-up following success. First, you were probably able to escape that first venture with a little cash. A first-time founder is often working amidst a frantic search for money, desperate for a paycheck, any paycheck, in order to escape sleeping in the broom closet. Going into a second venture following an exit will take off some of the pressure (you won't need quite so much ramen to get through the night).

Now, that being said, I would strongly caution you against over-investing in your new business. That pile of cash should be treated with venture-level restraint; think of your new business like an investor! Give your company a little seed money, and then force yourself to stay lean.

Another benefit of the second founding is (obviously) your newfound experience! While no two ventures are exactly alike, there will be some crossover and you will have some battle-tested lessons going forward. You will have a better handle on hiring (and firing), and will be more prepared for the gauntlet of pain that is fundraising. Your network will be deeper, you'll have some strong industry connections, and you might find it a little easier to do some basics (like recruit advisors, talent, investors, and customers).

You're a veteran now! You know what to do!

A final note on "the next big thing..."

Never forget how fun a start-up can be. Hidden amongst the panic, the pain, the tears, and the sweat and blood is an undercurrent of adventure. Building something from nothing is thrilling and satisfying, and even the angst and agony of failure and re-start can be curiously cleansing and beautiful.

As long as you're playing in the start-up game, always make sure you're enjoying yourself. If you wanted to have just another job, there are millions of places you can get one of those. A start-up is to be something special, something unique...

...something *you!*

FINAL THOUGHTS...

I've been circling around the start-up community in the Boston-Metro area for many years now, and the only pure truth I've uncovered is this:

The greatest feeling in life...

...is the feeling of **achievement**.

Get out there and do something.

Start something.

Struggle.

In the end, it'll all be worth it.

www.ingramcontent.com/pod-product-compliance
Lightning Source LLC
Chambersburg PA
CBHW071719170526
45165CB00005B/2080